Vie

a Lonely Planet travel atlas

Vietnam – travel atlas

1st edition

Published by
Lonely Planet Publications
Head Office: PO Box 617, Hawthorn, Vic 3122, Australia
Branches: 155 Filbert St, Suite 251, Oakland, CA 94607, USA
10 Barley Mow Passage, Chiswick, London W4 4PH, UK
71 bis rue du Cardinal Lemoine, 75005 Paris, France

Cartography by
Steinhart Katzir Publishers Ltd
Fax: 972-3-696 1360, 972-4-624975

Printed by
Colorcraft Ltd, Hong Kong

Photographs by
Glenn Beanland, Richard I'Anson, Brendan McCarthy, Helen Savory,
Robert Storey, Deanna Swaney

Front cover: Mui Ne Beach, South-Central Coast (Glenn Beanland)
Back cover: Basket vendor, Mekong Delta (Helen Savory)
Title page: Moored boats, Halong Bay (Richard I'Anson)

First Published
January 1996

**Although the authors and publisher have tried to make the information as
accurate as possible, they accept no responsibility for any loss, injury or
inconvenience sustained by any person using this book.**

National Library of Australia Cataloguing in Publication Data

Storey, Robert
Vietnam travel atlas.

1st ed.
Includes index.
ISBN 0 86442 367 5.

1. Vietnam – Maps, Tourist. 2. Vietnam – Road Maps.
I. Storey, Robert. (Series : Lonely Planet travel atlas).

912.597

Contents

Robert Storey

After graduating from the University of Nevada with a worthless liberal arts degree, Robert pursued a distinguished career as a slot machine repairman in a Las Vegas casino. He later worked for the government bureaucracy, though he is not quite sure what his job was. Seeking the meaning of life, Robert became a backpacker and drifted around Asia before he finally 'found himself'. These days he can mostly be found cruising the Internet.

Robert has worked on many Lonely Planet books, including guides to *China, Hong Kong, Macau & Canton* and *Taiwan*. He is the author of both the guide to *Vietnam* and the *Ho Chi Minh* city guide. He contributed his research skills once again to help produce the *Vietnam* travel atlas.

About this Atlas

This book is another addition to the Lonely Planet travel atlas series. Designed to tie in with the equivalent Lonely Planet guidebook, we hope the *Vietnam* travel atlas helps travellers enjoy their trip even more. As well as detailed, accurate maps, this atlas also contains a multilingual map legend, useful travel information in five languages, and a comprehensive index to ensure easy location-finding.

The maps were checked out by Robert Storey as part of preparation for a new edition of Lonely Planet's *Vietnam* guidebook.

From the Publishers

Thanks to Danny Schapiro, chief cartographer at Steinhart Katzir Publishers, who researched and drew the maps with the assistance of Liora Aharoni, and also to Mira Rotholtz who prepared the index. At Lonely Planet, the mapping was checked and index finalised by Lou Byrnes. Layout, design and cover design was completed by David Kemp. Thanks to Michelle Stamp for her overall assistance and to Claire Minty.

The language sections were coordinated with the assistance of Yoshiharu Abe, Pedro Diaz, Megan Fraser, Christine Gruettke, Sergio Mariscal, Isabelle Muller and Penelope Richardson.

Thanks also to Glenn Beanland and Linda Suttie for their willingness to help with tricky bits!

And of course, thanks to Robert Storey, for his thorough checking and patience.

Request

This atlas is designed to be clear, comprehensive and reliable. We hope you'll find it a worthy addition to your Lonely Planet travel library.

Even if you don't, please let us know! All suggestions and corrections are welcome – write to Lonely Planet and tell us what you think.

Vietnam

China

China

Tropic of Cancer

10 **11** **12** **13** **5**

Ha Giang

Lao Cai

Cao Bang

That Khe

14 **15** **16** Tuyen Quang Lang Son **17**

Yen Bai

Viet Tri Bac Ninh Bac Giang

Dien Bien Phu Son La **HANOI** Halong City

Ha Dong Hai Duong Cam Pha

Hoa Binh **HAIPHONG**

NAM DINH Thai Binh

Ninh Binh

Phat Diem **18** **19**

THANH HOA

Nghi Son Islands

Gulf of Tonkin

VINH

Hainan Island

Ha Tinh **20** **21**

Dong Hoi

Laos

Dong Ha

Thailand **22** Quang Tri **HUÉ** **23**

DANANG

Hoi An

Tam Ky

Quang Ngai

24 **25**

Kon Tum

Pleiku **QUI NHON**

Cambodia **26** **27** *South*

Buon Ma Thuot Tuy Hoa

Ninh Hoa *China*

DALAT **NHA TRANG**

Bao Loc **CAM RANH** *Sea*

28 **29** **30** **31**

Tay Ninh Phan Rang & Thap Cham

Thu Dau Mot **BIEN HOA**

HO CHI MINH (Saigon) Xuan Loc Phan Thiet

Chau Doc Cao Lanh Tan An Ba Ria Ham Tan

LONG XUYEN Ben Luc Long Dat

Ha Tien Vinh Long **MYTHO**

Phu Quoc Island Rach Gia Ben Tre **VUNG TAU**

32 Vi Thanh **CANTHO** **33**

Soc Trang Tra Vinh

Gulf of Thailand

Camau Bac Lieu *Con Dao Islands*

0 150 300 km

Northern Vietnam

Southern Vietnam

Thailand

Laos

Cambodia

Gulf of Thailand

South China Sea

Lao Bao
(Border Crossing)

Quang Tri

HUÉ

Cape Chan
May Dong

*Thua
Thien-Hue*

Hai Van
Pass

Son Cha Island
Cape Danang

DANANG
Hoi An

Cham Island
Ong Island

*Quang
Nam-
Danang*

Tam Ky

Cape An Hoa

Song Thinh

Song Khang

Dung Quat Bay
Cu Lao Re

Quang Ngai

Cape Batangan

*Quang
Ngai*

*Kon
Tum*

Kon Tum

Jrai Li Falls
(Thac Ya Li)

Pleiku

*Binh
Dinh*

Hon
Trau

An Khe
Pass

QUI NHON

*Gia
Lai*

Cu Mong
Pass

Lao
Ma N

Phu Yen

Lao
Duc

Tuy Hoa

Ba Krong

Buon Ma Thuot

Dac Lac
Lake

*Dac
Lac*

Hon G.
Peninsu
Van Phor
Bay
Hon Cha

Ninh Hoa

Khanh Hoa
NHA TRANG

Bamboo Isla
(Hon Tre)

DALAT

Ngoan
Muc Pass

CAM RANH

*Song
Be*

Nam Cat Tien
National Park

Lam Dong

Bao Loc

*Ninh
Thuan*

Cam Ra
Bay

14

Lien Khang
Waterfall

PHAN RANG & THAP CHAM

Cape Padaran

Padaran Bay

Tay Ninh

*Dong
Nai*

8

*Binh
Thuan*

Dau Tieng
Lake

Tay Ninh

Lake
Tri An

Phan Thiet

Moc Bai Border
Crossing

13

Lang a Lake

20

Phan Ri Bay

22

Thu Dau Mot

Xuan
Loc

Dong Thap

Long An

HO
Chi
Min

BIEN HOA
GIA
DINH

Mui Ne Point

Phan Thiet
Bay

Chau Doc

HO CHI MINH (Saigon)

Ben Luc

*Ba Ria-
Vung Tau*

Ham Tan

Ke Ga
Point

Cao Lanh

Tan An

Ba Ria

An Giang

LONG XUYEN

Tien Giang

Go Cong
Dong

Long
Dat

Ha Tien

Sa Dec

MYTHO

VUNG TAU

*Kien
Giang*

Vinh
Long

Ben Tre

Song Cua Dai

Hon Minh
Hoa

Rach Gia

CANTHO

Ben Tre

Song Ham Luong

Rach Gia
Bay

Vi Thanh

*Tra
Vinh*

Tra Vinh

Cung-Hau
Bay

Cantho

Ham
Rai

Soc Trang

Mekong
Delta

Rocher Table
Island

Soc Trang

Hau Giang
(Bassac River)

Poulo Dama

Hon
Rai

Poulo Panjang

Camau

Bac Lieu

Ngoc
Hien

Minh Hai

Hon Chuoi

Rocky Island
(Hon Buong)

Camau Nature Reserve

Con Dao
Islands

Con Son Island
Cau Island
Bay Canh Island

Cape Ca Mau

Poulo Obi
(Hon Khoai)

Hon Sao

Trung Lon
Island

Vung Island

Trung Nho
Island

Phu Quoc Island

Mekong River

0   100   200 km

MAP LEGEND

Number of Inhabitants:

HO CHI MINH		> 2,500,000
HAIPHONG	■	1,000,000 - 2,500,000
THAI NGUYEN	□	500,000 - 1,000,000
DANANG	◉	250,000 - 500,000
BIEN HOA	◎	100,000 - 250,000
Bac Ninh	◉	50,000 - 100,000
Bac Giang	◎	25,000 - 50,000
Hung Yen	◉	10,000 -25,000
Phu Binh	○	<10000
Lam Thao	◎	Village

HANOI Capital City
Capitale
Hauptstadt
Capital
首都

✪ Capital City (Locator map)
Capitale (Carte de situation)
Hauptstadt (Orientierungskarte)
Capital (Mapa Localizador)
首都 (地図上の位置)

QUI NHON Provincial Capital
Capitale de Province
Landeshauptstadt
Capital de Provincia
地方の中心地

International Boundary
Limites Internationales
Staatsgrenze
Frontera Internacional
国境

Provincial Boundary
Limites de la Province
Landesgrenze
Frontera de Provincia
地方の境界

Highway
Route Principale
Landstraße
Carretera
国道

Regional Road
Route Régionale
Regionale Fernstraße
Carretera Regional
地方道

Secondary Road
Route Secondaire
Nebenstraße
Carretera Secundaria
二級道路

Unsealed Road
Route non bitumée/piste
Unbefestigte Straße
Carretera sin Asfaltar
未舗装の道

Railway
Voie de chemin de fer
Eisenbahn
Ferrocarril
鉄道

4 Route Number
Numérotation Routière
Routenummer
Ruta Número
道路の番号

40 Distance in Kilometres
Distance en Kilomètres
Entfernung in Kilometern
Distancia en Kilómetros
距離 （km）

✈ International Airport
Aéroport International
Internationaler Flughafen
Aeropuerto Internacional
国際空港

✗ Domestic Airport
Aéroport National
Inlandflughafen
Aeropuerto Interior
国内線空港

☪ Mosque
Mosquée
Moschee
Mezquita
モスク

⊥ Temple
Temple
Tempel
Templo
寺院

† Cathedral
Cathédrale
Kathedrale
Catedral
大聖堂

ʃʃ Pass
Col
Paß
Desfiladero
峠

† Church
Église
Kirche
Iglesia
教会

National Park
Parc National
Nationalpark
Parque Nacional
国立公園

✕ Battle Site
Champ de Bataille
Schlachtstelle
Campo de Batalla
戰場

River
Fleuve/Rivière
Fluß
Río
川

Fort/Citadel
Château Fort/Citadelle
Festung/Zitadelle
Fuerte/Ciudadela
城・砦

Lake
Lac
See
Lago
湖

Ruins
Ruines
Ruinen
Ruinas
遺跡

Waterfall
Cascades
Wasserfall
Cascada
滝

Lighthouse
Phare
Leuchtturm
Faro
灯台

Swamp
Marais
Sumpf
Pantano
沼地

Seaport
Port de Mer
Seehafen
Puerto Marítimo
港

Tropics
Tropiques
Tropen
Los Trópicos
回帰線

Shipwreck
Épave
Schiffbruch
Naufragio
難破船

3500 m
3000 m
2500 m
2100 m

Beach
Plage
Strand
Playa
海岸

1800 m
1500 m
1200 m
900 m

Cave
Grotte
Höhle
Cueva
洞窟

600 m
450 m
300 m
150 m
0

Fansipan ✛
3143
Mountain
Montagne
Berg
Montaña
山

0   10   20   30   40   50 km

1 : 1 000 000

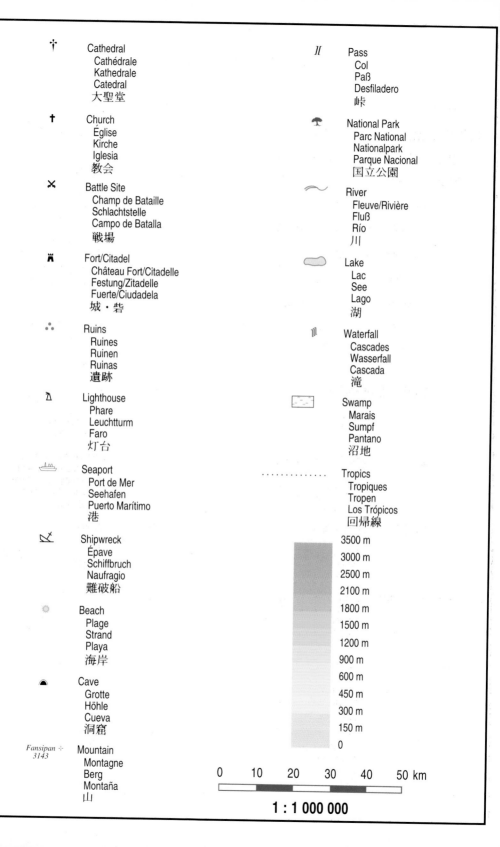

12

A   B   C   D

1

Kichou

Y u n n a n

Fuping

Napo

G u a n g x i

Song Mien

Mugang

Lung Cu

Donggan   ⊹ 1946   73

C h i n a

2

Zhendong

Ban Muong

Pho Bang

Dong Van

Songno

Meo Vac

Nanliangxu   Tancun

CHINA

Quan Ba   Cho Khem

Yen Minh

1691 ⊹

Ban Giay

Coc Pang

1152 ⊹

Bao Lac

1722 ⊹

Pac Bo   VIETNAM

Na Doc

Claire

95

1228 ⊹

Na Tom

Hang Pac Bo   Ha Quang

Thanh Thuy   24

2

Tsi Con Ling 2531 ⊹   **Ha Giang**   Vi Xuyen

Pac Mieu

Bac Me

1977 ⊹

Pac Tung

Nguyen Binh   3

Thong Nong

Na Giang

Nuoc Hai

3

H a G i a n g

Pa Pu

Tinh Tuc

1931 ⊹

Lang Vat   Ban Chong

Song Lo

Na Lanh

Phia Den ⊹ 1245

C a o B a n g

4

Bac Quang

1167 ⊹

Lung Gieng

Pac Vang

Ba Be Lake National Park   Song Nang

Cho Ra

Ngan Son

Viet Quang

178

Lung Minh

Na Hang

Ba Be Lake

Ba Be

1525 ⊹   Phu Thong

Na Phac

Nghia Phi

Vinh Tuy

Dai Thi

Cho Dien

192

Na Ri

5

Cham Chu 1595 ⊹

T u y e n

Cho Don

Bach Thong (Bac Can)

1086 ⊹

Elephant 1196 ⊹

Thac Cai

Chiem Hoa

Q u a n g

Ham Yen

Hoa Muc

Na Minh

Ven The

Thac Ba Lake

2

Ban Lap

B a c T h a i

Minh Lang

▼ 16 ▼

Cho Chu

6

Co Phuc

Yen Binh   958 ⊹

Tuyen Quang

Cho Moi

Trung Thanh

Hoa Trui

Tran Yen

Yen Son

Son Duong

Giang Tien

3

Vo Nhai

51

Song Day

Song Claire

165

Doan Hung

Tinh Sinh

1991 ⊹

Dai Tu

Bo Dau

Trung Cham

Trang Xa

Ca Vinh

Yen Bai

929 ⊹

THAI NGUYEN

Quynh Dong

18

14 1362 ⊹
Phou Tia
Lao Pie

A   B   C   D

Black River

1
Muang Va
Na Khoa
Pa Ham
96

Hat Sa
Ho Bay
Huoi Long

✈
Phongsali
Sung Ti Anh
6

VIETNAM
LAOS
Nam Mouk

Muang Hun
Xieng Hung
Na Lam
Muong Muon
Muong Ang
Tuan Giao

Nam Leng
Lai Chau

1686 ⊹
▲10▲

2
1771 ⊹
Sop Nhom
Co Cu

P h o n g s a l i
Ban Kha Na
105
Na La

Phia Lat
✈ ✕
Dien Bien Phu
Điện Biên Phủ

Sam Phan
Nam Noua
Ban Dan
Nam Ma

L a o s
Muang May
Tay Trang
1801 ⊹
Pa Thong

3
Muang Khua
424 ⊹
Sop At
Na Khoang
Nam Ma

Nam Ou
VIETNAM

Sin Xay
Pac Luong
Na Co
Sam Sao
1896 ⊹

Nam Pak
LAOS

Nam Lam
399 ⊹

4
Ban Na Tai
Pha Nang
Muang Po

Lao Sa
Muang Khao

Ban Na
Nambak
Muang Ngoi

L u a n g
P h a b a n g
Ban Se
Nam Seuang
Muang Xan

5
Nam Nga
Pac Lao
Muang Cut

Muang Sung
Ban Sop Tioc
Phou Loi
2252 ⊹

Nam Ou
Pa Phat
1826 ⊹

6
Mekong River
Pak Ou
Muang Hiem
Ha Tep

Ban Kho

Na Khang

Luang Phabang
Nam Ten
Pham Khao
Nam Khao

E · F · G · H

Lang Son
Lang Son

Cao Loc

Xieliang

C h i n a 1

Loc Binh

CHINA

VIETNAM

Song Ky Cung

Ban Chat

Po H

Lang Son

Na Duong

94

Hoanh Mo

Chi Lang

Khuoi Long

Dong Lac

71

Binh Lieu

Tan Mai

uu Lung

Luong Tam

▲13▲

Dinh Lap

Bac Moui

1259 ÷

Ha C

1

Luong Thuong

Khe Giam

4B

18

2

Trai Thuang

Chu

Song Luc Nam

Son Dong

Tien Yen

Dam Ha

Lang Giang

136

Ha Bac

740 ÷

Khe Trang

Ba Che

See inset

Dao Cai Chien

Luc Nam

Tan Dinh

An Leo

Phu Dien

Nam Vap 1045 ÷

Dao Sau Nam

Pha Lai

Chi Linh

Nam Mau 1067 ÷

Dong Vong

Dao Cai Bao

Q u a n g N i n h

Nga Hai

Mong Duong

Dao Tra Ban

Dao Dong Khoa

Dong Trieu

18

Uong Bi

Troi

62

Ha Tu

35

Cam Pha

Dao Co To

3

Mao Khe

18

Haiphong City West

Halong City East

361 ÷

Nam Thanh

45

5

Kim Mon

Thuy Nguyen

Quang Yen

Hang Dau Go Island (Ile des Merveilles)

Fat Tai Long Bay

Dao Trao

Hai Duong

Cam Binh

Tu Loc

HAIPHONG Hải Phòng

An Hai

Hang Dau Go Grotto ♠

Halong Bay Vinh Ha Long

Bo Han Island (Ile de la surprise)

Dao Ngoc Vung

Dao Quan Lan

Hung

Kien An

Haiphong

Fulong

Cat Ba Island

Cat Hai

Hang Trai Island (Ile de l'Union)

Dau Be Island

Dao Ha Mai

Quoc Coi

Tien Lang

Cat Ba National Park Công Viên Quốc Gia Cát Bà

Cat Ba

4

Vinh Bao

Do Son

Do Son Beach Bãi Biển Đồ Sơn

Phu Duc

River

Thai

Dao Long Chau

Dong Hung

Thai Thuy

Mouths Of The Red

G u l f o f T o n k i n

Binh

Thai Binh

D e l t a

China

Ngoc Cuc

Kien Xuong

Tien Hai

Jenyin Ling 714 ÷

5

Ha

Xuan Thuy

CHINA

Po Hen

Than Phun

VIETNAM

Hai Ninh

Donxing

▼19▼

Hoanh Mo

ai Hau

Binh Lieu

Tan Mai

1259 ÷

18

Ha Coi

Tien Yen

Dam Ha

Dao Vinh Thuc

6

Dao Cai Chien

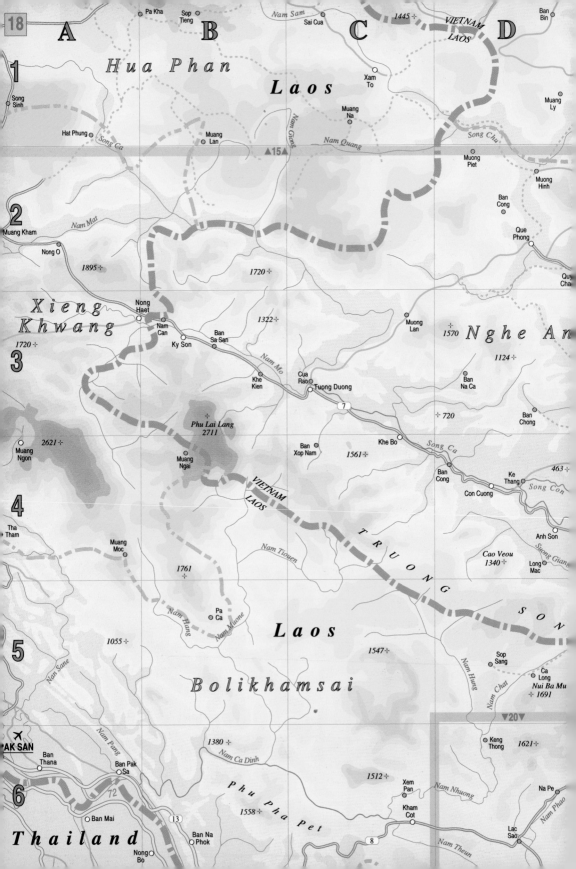

18

A   B   C   D

Hua Phan

1

Pa Kha   Sop Tieng   Nam Sam   Sai Cua   1445   **VIETNAM**   Ban Bin

LAOS

Song Sinh

Laos

Xam To   Muang Ly

Hat Phung   *Song Ca*   Muang Lan   Muang Na   Nam Quang   *Song Chu*

▲15▲   Muong Piet

Muong Hinh

2

Muang Kham   *Nam Mat*   Ban Cong

Nong O   1895 ✛   1720 ✛   Que Phong

Quy Chau

Xieng Khwang   Nong Haet   1322 ✛   Muong Lan   1570 ✛   *Nghe An*

3

1720 ✛   Nam Can   Ban Sa San   1124 ✛

Ky Son   *Nam Mo*   Khe Kien   Cua Rao   Ban Na Ca

Tuong Duong   ✛ 720   Ban Chong

7

Phu Lai Lang 2711   Ban Xop Nam   1561 ✛   Khe Bo   *Song Ca*

Muang Ngon   2621 ✛   Ban Cong   Ke Thang   463 ✛

Muang Ngai   Con Cuong   *Song Con*

4

Tha Tham   **VIETNAM LAOS**   Anh Son

Muang Moc   *Nam Tiouen*   *T R U O N G*   Cao Veou 1340 ✛   Long Mac

1761 ✛   *Suong Giang*

Pa Ca   *Nam Hang*   *S O N*

5

1055 ✛   *Nam Muone*   *Laos*   1547 ✛   Sop Sang

Nam Sane   Ca Long   *Nui Ba Mu* ✛ 1691

Bolikhamsai   *Nam Chat*   *Nam Hang*

▼20▼

✈ **AK SAN**   1380 ✛   Keng Thong   1621 ✛

Ban Thana   *Nam Pang*   *Nam Ca Dinh*   1512 ✛   Xem Pan   *Nam Nhuong*   Na Pe

Ban Pak Sa

6

72   *Phu Pha Pet*   Kham Cot   Lac Sao

Ban Mai   **13**   1558 ✛   **8**   *Nam Theun*   *Nam Phao*

Thailand   Ban Na Phok

Nong Bo

20

A

Keng Thong
1621

Na Pe

Lac Sao

Nam Nhuong

Nam Theun

▲18▲

1578

Na Va

Na Cang

Hin Bun

701

Ban Lao
787

Mahaxay

Tha Khaek
Nakhon Phanom

13

Bong Ca Xen

Tham Lay

Noong Booc

Na Sop
408

THAILAND

LAOS

13

Ban Khone Kene

Seno

Savannakhet

206

B

Ked Nua Pass

Nam Phao

Nam Sot

Rao Co
2286

Na Hao

Nam Theun

542

835

Na Kay

Nam One

Keng Cheng

Nhom Ma Lat

Nong Phao

Se Bang Fai

Nam La

440
Ban Van

247

Se Noi

Se Bang Fai

Na Kham

Phak Kha Nhia

Dong Hene

9

Se Champhone

Se Sang Soi

C

Yen Due

15

Phuong Dien

Huong Khe

Do Khe

Ngan Sau

Vang Sang

1938

Ca Xeng

Yen Lanh

12

Cha Lo

Mu Gia Pass

Long Khang

1512

Bua La Pha

Laos

Nha Vet
1385

Khammuan

Ca Vac

565

522

Na Nhom

Nam Pha Nang

Nam Tse

Ban Cang

Na Lai

Ma Pha Lan
438

Xa Nun

Se Kun Kam

D

Can Loc

Ngoc My

45

Thach Ha

Ha Tinh
● Hà Tĩnh

Ha Tinh

Cam Xuyen
Cẩm Xuyên

1

Phuor Giai

Tuy Loc

Bai Duc Thon

Vong Lieu

645

Thanh Lang

Nguon Nay

Minh Hoa

15

890
Cha Noi

Quang

1074

S O N

848

VIETNAM

LAOS

Muang Xen

Ban Bung

Se Nam Kok

809

Tha Mo

At Lam

Muang Phin

Numbered rows

1

2

3

4

5

Savannakhet

6

Cape Mui Ron

Ky Anh

Phuc San

1007 ⊹

Đèo Ngàng (Ngang Pass)
Đèo Ngang

Hung Son

Canh Duang

Quang Trach

Song Giang

Ba Don

Quang Khe

Phong Nha Cave
Dong Phong Nha

Son Trach

Bo Trach

Nhat Le Beach

15

1137 ⊹

Phu Quy

Rau Nhat

Dong Hoi
Đồng Hới

Le Ninh

Ben Triem

B i n h

Lang Mo

Dai Giang

Kien Giang

Xuan Hoa

Thach Ban

53   Le Thuy

1

Ba Binh

Cape Lay

Con Co

Gulf
of
Tonkin

M
O
U
N
T
A
I
N
S

1272 ⊹

Vit Thu Lu

Phuong Lieu

Ben Quang

Ban Hai

Vinh Moc Tunnels

Cua Tung Beach

Truong Son
National Cemetery

Ben Hai River

41

Vu Con

Gio Linh

Cua Viet Beach

812

Se Bang Hieng

Ban Co

Huong Lap

Song Cam Lo

Cam Lo

9

13

Dong Ha
Đồng Hà

Gia Dang Beach

VIETNAM

LAOS

1701

▼**22**▼

Q u a n g   T r i

80

Ca Lu

Ba Long

Quang Tri
Quảng Trị

Song Cua Ha

Hai Lang

Dien Mon

Ban Dong

Lao Bao (Border Crossing)
Lao Bảo

Khe Sanh

✕

Huong Hoa

Dakrong Bridge
Cầu Đắk Rông

Song Quang Tri

268 ⊹

56

Tchepone River (Song Xe Pone)

730 ⊹

14

Dakrong River

1102 ⊹

Huong Dien

1

Quang Dien

Phu Vang

Thuan An Beach

Ban Lao

A Dong

Co Bi

Huong Tra

HUE
Hue

Huong Phu

*South
China
Sea*

Vinh
Loc
*Cape Chan
May Dong*

*Dam
Cau Hai*

Truoi

Phu
Gia

Lang Co
Lang Co

Son Cha Island

Phu
Loc

Hai Van Pass
Đèo Hai Van

25

*Bay of
Danang*

**Nam O
Beach**

Nui Son Tra

Cape Danang

**Bach Ma
tional Park**

Bach
Ma

Song Nam O

Nam O

Thanh Binh Beach

My Khe Beach

1707

Hoa
Vang

● **DANANG
Đà Nẵng**

Ba Na

Hue
Duc

China Beach

Cham Island

*Marble
Mountains*

Song
Kon

Ha Tan

Dai Loc

Dien
Ban

**Cua Dai
Beach**

**Hoi An
Hội An**

Ong Island

ong Bung

An Hoa

Duy Xuyen

**My Son
Mỹ Sớn**

791

ong Cai

Thang
Binh

Giang

1142

Nong
San

845

Que Son

14

Song Tranh

Hiep
Duc

Song Rhang

677

**Tam Ky
Tam Kỳ**

Cape An Hoa

Phuoc
Hao

Gia Ngan
Duoi

Q u a n g

Tien
Phuoc

69

*Dung Quat
Bay*

Chu Lai

Cape Nam Tram

Phuoc
Son

N a m - D a n a n g

Bong
Mieu

Song Quan

1

Cu Lao Re

Thon
Bon

Tra My

*Ngoc Chua
1362*

Binh
Khuong

Son
Tra

Phuoc
Cong

*Hon Ba
1356*

Tra
Giac

Tra
Phong

Tra
Bong

Binh Son

*ak
u*

2047

Nam Nun

Ba Gia

Son
Tinh

Tinh
Hoa

**Bien Khe
Ky Beach**

Cape Batangan

ac Glei

**My Lai
(Son My)**

Ngoc
Linh

Mang
Ri

Mang
Xim

**Quang Ngai
Quang Ngãi**

Tu
Nghia

2598
*Ngoc Linh
Mountain*

▼24▼

▼25▼

Kon Tum

Tu Mo
Rong

Dac
A Koi

2025

Mang
Buk

Dak Dein

Son Ha

Ta
Bien

Quang Ngai

Minh
Long

Manh
Tin

Nghia
Hanh

Mo Duc

Duc
Lam

Dak To

Gia
Vuc

Ba To

Ba
Dong

Song Ve

753

Liet
Son

Duc Pho

Sa Huynh
Sa Huynh

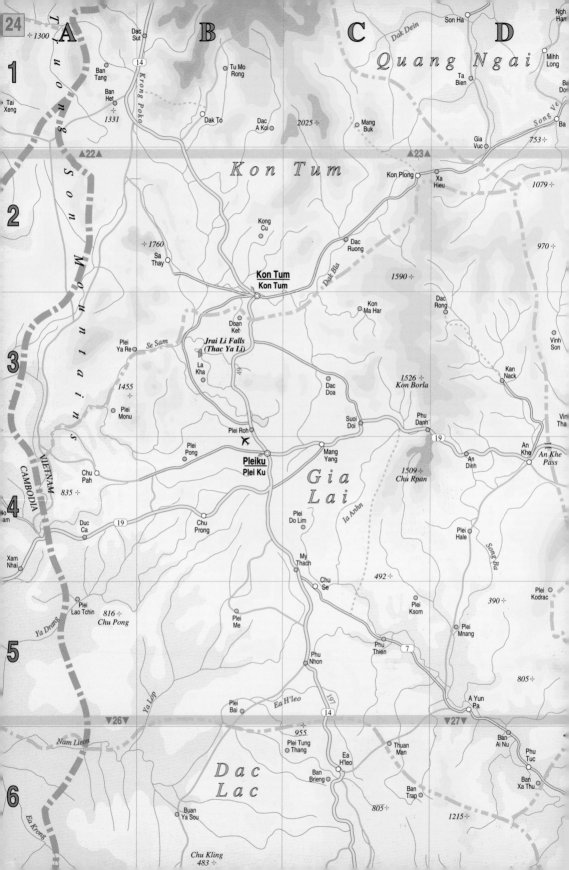

A   B   C   D

1

2

3

4

5

6

÷ 1300

Tuong Son Mountains

Dac Sut

Ban Tang

Tai Xeng

Ban Het
÷ 1331

14

Krong Poko

Tu Mo Rong

Dak To

Dac A Koi

2025 ÷

Kon Tum

Son Ha

Dak Dein

Ta Bien

Minh Long

Ngh Han

Quang Ngai

Mang Buk

Gia Vuc

753 ÷

Ba

Son Ve

Ba Doi

▲22▲   ▲23▲

Kong Cu

÷ 1760

Sa Thay

Kon Plong

Xa Hieu

1079 ÷

Dac Ruong

970 ÷

Se Sam

Kon Tum
Kon Tum

Dak Bla

1590 ÷

Dac Rong

Plei Ya Re

Doan Ket

Jrai Li Falls
(Thac Ya Li)

La Kha

49?

Kon Ma Har

1526 ÷
Kon Borla

Vinh Son

Kan Nack

Vin Tha

1455 ÷

Plei Monu

Dac Doa

Suoi Doi

Phu Danh

An Khe

An Khe Pass

Plei Roh

Plei Pong

Pleiku
Plei Ku

Mang Yang

19

An Dinh

Chu Pah

835 ÷

Gia Lai

1509 ÷
Chu Rpan

Duc Ca

19

Chu Prong

Plei Do Lim

Ia Anun

Plei Hale

Song Ba

Xam Nhai

My Thach

492 ÷

390 ÷

Plei Kodrac

VIETNAM
CAMBODIA

Plei Lao Tchin

816 ÷
Chu Pong

Plei Me

Chu Se

Plei Ksom

Plei Mnang

Ya Drang

Phu Thien

7

805 ÷

Phu Nhon

A Yun Pa

Ya Lop

▼26▼   ▼27▼

Plei Bai

Ea H'leo

14

197

Nam Lieon

955

Plei Tung Thang

Ban Brieng

Ea H'leo

Thuan Man

Ban Ai Nu

Phu Tuc

Ea Krong

Dac Lac

Buan Ya Sou

Ban Trap

805 ÷

Ban Xa Thu

1215 ÷

Chu Kling
483 ÷

E   **F**   **G**   **H**

1

2

3

4

5

6

Mo Duc

Duc Lam

Duc Pho

Liet Son

Sa Huynh
Sa Huynh

▲23▲

An Lao

Tam Quan

An Hoa

Hoai Nhon

Song Lon

Hoai An

My Loc

Nghia Dien

My Tho

Hon Trau

Binh Dinh

Phu My

Trinh Khanh

Cat Hanh

Phu Cat

Vinh Son Falls

Phu Phong   19

Cha Ban

Binh Dinh

Tuy Phuoc

Thap Doi   **QUI NHON**
Qui Nhón

Cape Hirondelles

Hon Cohe

South China Sea

Cu Mong Pass

Cu Mong

1146

Cu Lao Xanh

Van Canh

Xuan Lanh

Song Cau

Phu Giang

Xuan Thinh

1284
Chu Nhon

Dong Xuan

Chao Bay

▼27▼

Chi Thanh

Phu Yen

Tuy An

Lao Ma Nha

Tan Hoi

San Long

Lao Dua

Son Hoa   7

Tuy Hoa
Tuy Hòa

Xuan Duc

Song Ba

Song Hinh

Van An

Ban Thach

A B C D

1

Nam Lieon

Ea H'leo

Dak Rouei

Dak Kroeng

Co Nhec

Ea Krong

Buan
Ya Sou

Chu Kling
483 ✛
▲24▲

2

Mondulkin

Ro Mat

Dak Plai

Ban Drang
Phok

Ea Sup

Chu Don
491 ✛

Ban
Don

Bet
Chan Da

Dak
Nam

Keo
So Ma

Dak Dam

Dray
Ling

*Drai Sap
Falls*

Cambodia

Krong
Te

Senmonorom

Dak
Gang

Buc
Tu

3

Xre
Khotong

Buy
Phloc

Pu
Kle

Dac
Dam

Dak
Mil

Kri
A

Ô Rang

Dao
Thong

Duc
Xuyen

✛ 1544

4

Xre
Khotum

Bu
Prang

Tuy
Duc

*Dac
Lac*

Bon Bu
Tong

CAMBODIA
VIETNAM

Bu Gia
Map

Doan
Van

880 ✛

Lo
Nghiem

Bu
Blim

Kien
Duc

Dak
Nong

Bu
Dop

Bu
Xa

Dak Glun

Bich
Son

Lac
Thanh

*Song
Be*

Dac
Kla

Phuoc
Long

Dak Rlap

Bu
Dang

Buon
Sop

Dak Deung

Loc
Ninh

Song Be

5

Bu
Nho

14

Cat
Tien

*Nam Cat Tien
National Park*

*Dambri
Falls*

▼30▼

▼31▼

An Loc

Phu
Rieng

Bu
Na

Bu
Go

Bao Loc
Bảo Lộc ✝

Thuan
Loi

Tan
Khai

Da
Te

Da Te

Dai
Lao

Song
Be

Dong
Xoai

Song Be

Da Huoai

1088 ✛

20

6

Chon
Thanh

*Dong
Nai*

Dong Nai

Phuong
Lam

Bau
Long

Phuoc
Vinh

Rang
Rang

Song Mada

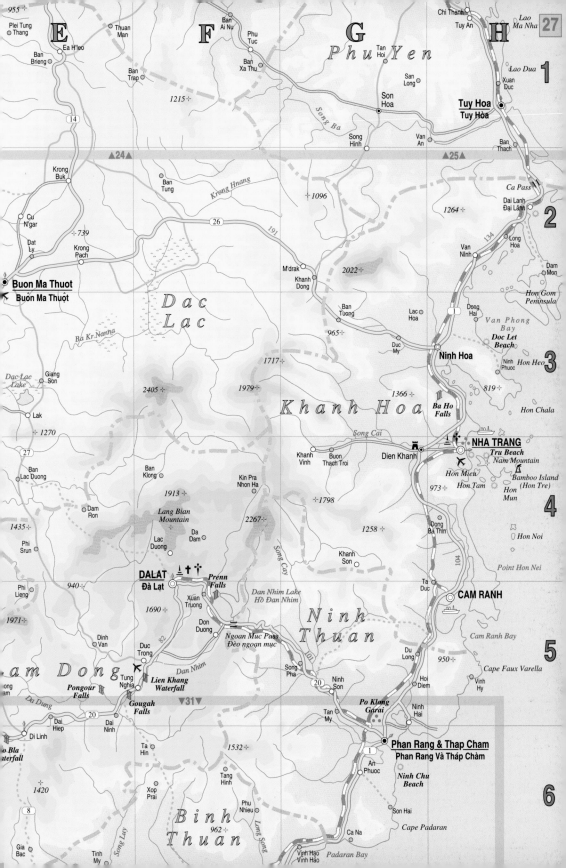

E   **F**   **G**   **H**

1

2

3

4

5

6

Pe Rang
Con Chai Mia
Xa Mat
Tan Lon
Bau Tram

Pray Veng

Pray Veng

Tan Phu
Tan Bien

Tay Ninh

Lo Go

Sa Ang

1

Rome Hec

Nui Ba Den
(Black Lady Mountain)
850 +

Long Hon

Cang Dan

Banam

Svay Rieng

Hoa Thanh

Dau Tieng Lake

Song Sai Gon

Tri Tam

Chau Thanh
Tay Ninh

Loc Dec

Rum Duon

22

Ben Cui

Ben Suc

Prek Trabek 125

Khiem Hanh

Piem Cho

Kompong Trabek

Cham Calieu

Svay Rieng

36

1
58

Moc Bai Border Crossing

Go Dau

Trang Bang

Svay Tep

CAMBODIA
VIETNAM

Se So Thuong

Cai Cai

Long Khot

Vinh Hung

Duc Hue

Hiep Hoa

Hau Nghia

Hong Ngu

Long An

Mat Cat

Duc Hoa

30

Phu Chau

Dong Bac Chien

Moc Hoa

West Vaico

Tan Buu

au Doc

Hoa Binh

An Long

Thanh Binh

Thanh Loi

Tuyen Nhen

Sam Mountain
g

Chau Phu

Phu Tan

Dong Thap

Kinh Cung

Tan Thanh

Ap Bac

Thu Thua

Bin Hung

Hoa Hao

Tam Nong

Tan Dong

My Chanh

Tan An

1

h Bien

Chau Thanh

Cho Moi

An Phu

Thap Muoi

Tien Giang

Chau Thanh

An

Chau Thanh

30

Cao Lanh

My Dien

Cai Lay

Cho Gao

Cau Sac

91

Giang

LONG XUYEN

Thanh Hung

Khanh An

Tien Giang River
(Upper Mekong River)

Cai Be

Dong Tam
Snake Farm

MYTHO
Mỹ Tho

Co To

Tay An

Sa Dec
Sa Đéc

Chau Thanh

My Thuan

Vinh Long
Vĩnh Long

Chau Thanh

Ba The

Thoai Son

Thot Not

Tan An

Phu Binh

Cho Lach

Cai Mon

Ben Tre

80

Cai San

91

O Mon

Hau Giang (Bassac)

Long Ho

Mang Thit

Ben Tre

Rach Gia
Rạch Giá

Phu Hoi

Tan Hiep

Thanh Loi

Thoi Hoa

CANTHO
Cần Thơ

Binh Minh

Phu Quy

Tam Binh

Vinh

Vung Liem

Mo Cay

Phang Dien

Cai Rang

1

Long

Hun Nha
Huang My

Chau Thanh

Hoa Binh

Giong Rieng

Ngoc Loi

Chau Thanh

Tra On

Cang Long

Tra Vinh

Kien An

12

Ben Nhurt

32

33

Chau Thanh

Vinh Cui

Tra

Mekong

Vi Thanh

Thuan Nham

Rach Goi

Phung Hiep

Cau Ke

Tieu Can

Dau Giong

Vinh

Delta

Go Quao

Duc Long

My Hoa

Floating Market

Ke Sach

Mac Bac

Dai Ngai

Tra Cu

Cau Ngang

Vinh Hoa

Long My

1

E   F   G   H

1

Dambri
Falls

ao Lộc
ảo Lộc †

Dai
Lao

20

Lien
Dam

49

Di Linh

**Bo Bla
Waterfall**

Da Dung

Dai
Hiep

Dai
Ninh

Tung
Nghia

Ta
Hin

Xop
Prai

Lam Dong

1420 ÷

8

Ninh
Son

Tan
My

20

Ninh
Hai

Phan Rang & Thap Cham
Phan Rang Và Tháp Chàm

An
Phuoc

1

*Ninh Chu
Beach*

Son Hai

1532 ÷

Tang
Hinh

Phu
Nhieu

962 ÷

Long Song

Ca Na

Cape Padaran

2

Gia
Bac

An Lam

Tinh
My

Song Luy

Song
Mao

Bac
Binh

Phan
Ri Cua

Vinh Hao
Vinh Hảo

Padaran Bay

Tuy
Phong

▲26▲

146

Phan Ri Bay

▲27▲

Suong Katok

1229 ÷

Nui Ong

**Binh
Thuan**

Ham
Thuan Bac

Long
Lam

Thien
Ai

3

Muong
Man

Binh
Lam

Song
Phan

1

Ham
Ninh

**Phan Thiet
Beach**

Phan Thiet
Phan Thiet

Hai
Long

Mui
Ne

Mui Ne Point

*Mui Ne
Beach*

*Phan Thiet
Bay*

Tan
Thuan

Song Phan

Ke Ga Point

Ham Tan

4

South China Sea

5

6

T r a E *Vinh* F G H

Tra Vinh

Cang Long

1

Chau Thanh

Cau Ke

Tieu Can

Vinh Cuu

Thanhphu

Mekong

Mac Bac

Dau Giong

Delta

Cau Ngang

Thanh Phuoc

Dai Ngai

Tra Cu

Long Phu

Cung-Hau Bay

Song Co Chien

Song Ham Luong

▲29▲

Soc Trang
Sóc Trăng

Long Phu

Dai An

Duyen Hai

▲30▲

Mouths of the Mekong

My Xuyen

Lich Hoi Thuong

Hau Giang (Bassac River)

2

Ben Pha

Lai Hoa

Vinh Chau

S o u t h
C h i n a
S e a

3

4

Con Dao Islands
Côn Đảo

Tre Nho Island

Dong Bac Point

Tre Lon Island

Con Son Island

Ba Island

Con Dao

Cau Island

Bay Canh Island

Vung Island

Ca Map Point

Trung Lon Island

Trac Island

Tho Island

Trung Nho Island

5

6

Getting Around Vietnam

Bus

The good news is that Vietnam has an extensive network of dirt-cheap buses which reach virtually every corner of the country. The bad news is that buses tend to be slow, crowded, uncomfortable and subject to frequent breakdowns. Most bus drivers stop frequently to pick up and discharge passengers all along the route. This not only causes frustrating delays, but also means the bus tends to get more and more crowded as the journey progresses. In theory you can purchase two tickets which entitles you to twice as much legroom, but in practice you may have a difficult time defending your turf from invading passengers. There is scant space for luggage and you may have to store your bag on the roof of the bus, which means you won't have access to it during the trip.

Minibuses are another option – they tend to be more comfortable and faster. There are two types of minibuses – public and chartered ones. The public minibuses are scaled-down versions of the large buses – they pick up passengers all along the route and can become very crowded and uncomfortable. Chartered minibuses are supposedly not permitted to cram in extra passengers, but of course you pay more for the luxury. You can easily book seats on these chartered vehicles at cafes, hotels and travel agencies that cater to foreigners or well-to-do Vietnamese.

Train

Most of Vietnam's 2600-km railway system consists of a single line running the length of the country between Hanoi and Saigon (1726 km). From Hanoi there are also three spur lines – two lines to the Chinese border and one to the port of Haiphong.

Air-conditioned sleeping berths are obtainable on the 'Reunification Express' trains which link Saigon to Hanoi. However, local trains can be excruciatingly slow and uncomfortable, and there is a problem with luggage theft.

There are different classes offering a wide range of price possibilities and standards of comfort.

Car

Self-drive car rentals have yet to make their debut in Vietnam, but hiring a car or minibus with a driver is so cheap that it's worth considering. Indeed, given the decrepit condition of Vietnam's public transport, travelling by rented car is a very popular option. Splitting the

HELEN SAVORY

Long Hai Beach, near Vung Tau, South Coast

tariff between a small group of travellers reduces the cost even further, sometimes to as little as US$5 per day.

All sorts of travel agencies in Hanoi and Saigon can arrange a customised tour of the country with a private car, driver and translator/guide. The cost per km varies from around US$0.30 to US$0.70 depending on the size of the vehicle. You may or may not be responsible for paying the wages of the guide and driver (perhaps US$5 per day per person) plus their accommodation and meal costs – make sure this is cleared up before you set out. In many cases you will be quoted an all-inclusive cost per day which even includes accommodation in a budget hotel. Although not mandatory, if you receive good service from your driver and guide, a tip would be most appreciated.

Bicycle

Touring Vietnam by bicycle is eminently possible, but the biggest challenge is planning a route that avoids the murderous traffic. Areas to avoid include the Mekong Delta and National Highway 1. Many cyclists are most enthralled about Highway 14 which runs through the Central Highlands of the south (around Buon Ma Thuot). Highway 7, which runs from Hanoi to the Chinese border at Lao Cai, also gets goods reviews.

You can purchase low-quality mountain bikes in Hanoi and Saigon, but most cyclists prefer to bring their own.

Boat

Extended boat journeys are most practical in the Mekong Delta region of southern Vietnam, which is criss-crossed with hundreds of rivers and canals. However, there are popular scenic day tours to visit offshore islands, especially from Nha Trang and in Halong Bay.

DEANNA SWANEY

RICHARD I'ANSON

BRENDAN McCARTHY

Top: Floating homes, Langa Lake, Central Highlands
Middle: Buying bread, Cholon Market, Ho Chi Minh City
Bottom: Street scene, Ho Chi Minh City

Comment Circuler au Vietnam

FRANÇAIS
Bus

La bonne nouvelle, c'est que le Vietnam dispose d'un vaste réseau de bus très peu chers desservant pratiquement les quatre coins du pays. La mauvaise, c'est qu'ils sont plutôt lents, bondés, inconfortables et victimes de fréquentes pannes. La plupart s'arrêtent régulièrement pour prendre et déposer des voyageurs, ce qui entraîne des retards sur l'horaire initial. Théoriquement, vous pouvez acheter deux billets afin de pouvoir étendre vos jambes mais, dans la pratique, il est difficile de défendre son territoire. Naturellement il y a peu de place pour les bagages et vous devrez vraisemblablement installer les vôtres sur le toit ; ce qui signifie que vous n'y aurez pas accès durant le trajet.

Vous pouvez également opter pour le minibus, généralement plus confortable et plus rapide. Il en existe deux catégories : les publics et les charters. Les premiers sont des versions bas de gamme des bus normaux : ils prennent des passagers tout au long de la route et finissent bondés et inconfortables. Les bus charters, qui n'ont (normalement) pas le droit de prendre de voyageurs supplémentaires, sont plus chers. Vous pouvez réserver vos places dans les agences de voyages, les cafés et les hôtels fréquentés par les étrangers et les Vietnamiens aisés.

Train

La majeure partie du réseau ferré, qui couvre 2600 km, consiste en une ligne unique traversant le pays dans le sens de la longueur entre Hanoi et Saigon (1726 km). Il existe également trois lignes transversales au départ d'Hanoi, dont deux à destination de la frontière chinoise, la troisième desservant le port de Haiphong.

Sur les trains 'Reunification express' reliant Saigon à Hanoi, il est possible de voyager en couchette climatisée. En revanche, les trains locaux peuvent être extrêmement lents et inconfortables. Les vols de bagages sont par ailleurs très fréquents.

Il existe de différentes classes offrant une gamme de prix et un niveau de confort variés.

Voiture

S'il est désormais possible de louer un véhicule particulier sans chauffeur au Vietnam, la location d'un minibus ou d'une voiture avec chauffeur coûte si peu cher que cela vaut la peine d'y réfléchir. De toutes façons, compte tenu de l'état de décrépitude des transports publics vietnamiens, la location de voitures semble ne présenter que des avantages. En parta-

RICHARD I'ANSON

Woman rowing boat, Halong Bay

RICHARD I'ANSON

DEANNA SWANEY

Top: Junks and boats, Halong Bay
Bottom: Marble Mountains, near Danang

geant les frais avec un petit groupe de voyageurs, cela peut revenir à environ 5 $US par jour seulement.

Pratiquement toutes les agences de voyages de Saigon et d'Hanoi proposent des circuits sur mesure en voiture particulière avec chauffeur et guide/interprète. Le prix du kilomètre varie entre 0,30 $US et 0,70 $US environ, en fonction de la taille du véhicule. Les salaires du guide et du chauffeur (environ 5 $US par jour chacun), de même que leur hébergement et leurs repas, n'étant pas toujours compris, soumettez la question à l'agence avant votre départ. La plupart du temps on vous indiquera un prix net par jour, comprenant une chambre dans un hôtel de classe économique. Bien que cela ne soit pas obligatoire, n'oubliez pas de donner un pourboire au chauffeur et au guide lorsqu'ils vous ont donné satisfaction.

Bicyclette

Il est tout à fait possible de visiter le Vietnam à vélo, mais il faut pouvoir établir un itinéraire permettant d'éviter les voies à grande circulation. Le trafic est particulièrement dangereux dans le delta du Mekong ainsi que sur la Nationale 1.

De nombreux cyclistes ont été séduits par la Nationale 14 qui traverse les plateaux du sud (environs de Buon Ma Thuot).

La Nationale 7 qui relie Hanoi à Lao Kay, à la frontière chinoise, semble également très appréciée.

Vous pouvez acheter des VTT bas de gamme à Hanoi et Saigon, mais la plupart des cyclistes préfèrent emporter leur propre matériel.

Bateau

Le bateau est un moyen de transport particulièrement pratique dans le delta du Mekong, au sud du Vietnam, car la région est parcourue de centaines de rivières et de canaux. Des circuits touristiques sont organisés dans les îles situées au large des côtes, notamment à Nha Trang et dans la baie d'Along.

Reisen in Vietnam

DEUTSCH
Per Bus

Zwar verfügt Vietnam über ein ausgedehntes und dabei spottbilliges Busnetz, das dem Reisenden praktisch alle Ecken des Landes erschließt, doch sind Busse im allgemeinen langsam, überfüllt, unbequem und ausgesprochen pannenfreundlich. Die meisten Busfahrer halten oft für Passagiere entlang der gesamten Strecke, was die Reise nicht nur frustrierend verzögert, sondern auch bedeutet, daß der Bus oft im Laufe der Reise immer voller wird. Theoretisch kann man zwei Fahrkarten und damit zweimal so viel Platz für die Beine kaufen, doch dürfte es in der Praxis schwierig sein, dieses 'Revier' gegen andere Passagiere zu verteidigen. Für Gepäck gibt es kaum Platz, so daß die Tasche meist auf dem Busdach verstaut wird – was bedeutet, daß man während der ganzen Reise nicht an sie heran kann.

Minibusse sind eine weitere Möglichkeit – sie sind oft bequemer und schneller. Es gibt zwei Arten von Minibussen – öffentliche und gecharterte. Die öffentlichen Minibusse sind kleinere Versionen der großen Busse – sie nehmen Passagiere entlang der gesamten Route auf und können äußerst voll und unbequem werden. Gecharterte Minibusse dürfen angeblich keine zusätzlichen Passagiere aufnehmen, doch zahlt man für diesen Luxus selbstverständlich auch mehr. Plätze in diesen gecharterten Bussen sind einfach in Cafés, Hotels und Reisebüros zu buchen, die auf Ausländer oder wohlhabende Vietnamesen zugeschnitten sind.

Per Zug

Der Großteil von Vietnams 2600 km umfassenden Schienensystem besteht aus einer einzigen Linie, die die gesamte Länge des Landes zwischen Hanoi und Saigon (1726 km) versorgt. Von Hanoi aus gibt es dazu drei Nebenlinien, zwei zur chinesischen Grenze und eine zum Hafen von Haiphong.

Klimatisierte Schlafkabinen sind in 'Reunification Express'-Zügen erhältlich, die Saigon mit Hanoi verbinden. Dagegen können Nahverkehrszüge entsetzlich langsam und unbequem sein, und obendrein stellt Gepäckdiebstahl ein großes Problem dar.

Verschiedene Klassen bieten dem Touristen vielerlei Preisoptionen und Komfortklassen.

Per Auto

Self-Drive-Autovermietungen müssen noch ihr Debut in Vietnam machen, doch ist das Mieten eines Autos oder Minibusses mit Fahrer so billig, daß sich lohnt, diese Möglichkeit in Erwägung zu ziehen. In Anbetracht des altersschwachen vietnamesischen öffentlichen Transportsystems ist das Reisen im Mietwagen sehr beliebt. Kostenteilung in einer kleinen Reisegruppe senkt die Kosten in manchen Fällen sogar bis auf nur US$ 5 pro Tag.

Alle möglichen Reisebüros in Hanoi und Saigon können kundenspezifische Touren mit

ROBERT STOREY

Traditional fishing, Mekong Delta

Privatwagen, Fahrer und Übersetzer/Fremdenführer arrangieren. Die Kosten pro Kilometer schwanken abhängig von der Fahrzeuggröße zwischen etwa US$ 0,30 bis US$ 0,70. Es mag Ihnen obliegen, oder auch nicht, das Gehalt des Fremdenführers und Fahrers (vielleicht US$ 5 pro Tag pro Person) plus deren Unterkunfts- und Verpflegungskosten zu bezahlen. Stellen Sie sicher, daß diese Frage vor Reiseantritt geklärt ist. In vielen Fällen wird man Ihnen eine Tageskostenpauschale angeben, die sogar die Unterkunft in einem Budget-Hotel beinhaltet. Obwohl nicht vorgeschrieben, kommen Trinkgelder an Fahrer und Fremdenführer für gute Dienste immer gut an.

Per Fahrrad

Vietnam mit dem Fahrrad zu bereisen, ist zwar ausgezeichnet möglich, doch liegt die größte Herausforderung in der Planung einer Route, die den mörderischen Verkehr umgeht. Zu vermeiden sind u. a. das Mekong-Delta und der National Highway 1.

Viele Radfahrer sind vom Highway 14 höchst begeistert, der durch das zentrale Hochland im Süden (um Buon Ma Thuot) führt. Der von Hanoi zur chinesischen Grenze bei Lao Cai verlaufende Highway 7 ist ebenfalls sehr beliebt.

Zwar sind Tourenräder bescheidener Qualität in Hanoi und Saigon erhältlich, doch bevorzugen die meisten Radfahrer ihre eigene Ausrüstung.

Per Schiff

Ausgedehnte Schiffsreisen unternimmt man am besten im Gebiet des Mekong-Deltas in Südvietnam, das von hunderten von Flüssen und Kanälen durchzogen ist. Besonders in Nha Trang und Halong Bay werden populäre Tagestouren zu vor der Küste gelegenen Inseln angeboten.

BRENDAN McCARTHY

GLENN BEANLAND

BRENDAN McCARTHY

Top: Concert, School of Art, Ho Chi Minh City
Middle: Long Xuyen Market, Mekong Delta
Bottom: Mending fishing nets, Nha Trang, South-Central Coast

Cómo Movilizarse dentro de Vietnam

ESPAÑOL

En Autobús

La buena noticia es que Vietnam tiene una extensa red de autobuses, increíblemente baratos, que llegan prácticamente a todos los rincones del país. La mala noticia es que los autobuses generalmente son lentos, apiñados, incómodos y paran frecuentemente. La mayoría de los conductores de autobuses se detienen muchas veces para que suban y bajen los pasajeros a lo largo de la ruta. Esto no solamente causa retrasos frustrantes, sino que también el autobús se apiña cada vez más a medida que transcurre el viaje. En teoría, uno puede comprar dos pasajes, lo que le daría derecho a doble espacio para estirar las piernas, pero en la práctica es difícil defender el espacio contra los pasajeros invasores. El espacio para el equipaje es muy escaso y puede que uno tenga que colocarlo sobre el techo del autobús, lo que quiere decir que no tendrá acceso al mismo durante el viaje.

Otra alternativa son los minibuses que por lo general son más cómodos y más rápidos. Hay dos tipos de minibuses: los públicos y los de alquiler. Los minibuses públicos son versiones más pequeñas de los autobuses grandes; estos recogen pasajeros a lo largo de la ruta y pueden llegar a estar muy apiñados e incómodos. Supuestamente, en los minibuses de alquiler no está permitido apiñar pasajeros adicionales, pero naturalmente hay que pagar más por este lujo. Se pueden reservar fácilmente asientos en estos minibuses de alquiler en cafés, hoteles y agencias de viajes que atienden a los extranjeros y a los vietnamitas de buenos recursos económicos.

En Tren

La mayor parte de los 2600 km de línea ferroviaria de Vietnam consiste en una línea que va a lo largo del país entre Hanoi y Saigón (1736 km). Desde Hanoi hay solamente tres líneas secundarias: dos que van a la frontera con China y una que va al puerto de Haiphong.

Se pueden obtener cabinas dormitorio con aire acondicionado en los trenes 'Expreso de la Reunificación' que unen a Saigón con Hanoi. Sin embargo, los trenes locales pueden ser extremadamente lentos e incómodos y se presentan muchos problemas con el robo de equipajes.

En los trenes se ofrecen varias clases con distintos precios y niveles de comodidad.

En Automóvil

El alquiler de automóviles para conducirlos uno mismo todavía no ha hecho su debut en Vietnam, pero el alquilar un automóvil o minibús con chofer es tan barato, que vale la pena considerlo. Realmente, dada la condición decrépita del transporte público de Vietnam, el viajar en automóviles alquilados es una opción muy popular. El dividir el costo entre un pequeño grupo de viajeros reduce el costo aún más, en al-

RICHARD I'ANSON

Junks moored in Halong Bay

gunos casos puede ser de sólo $5 dólares por día.

Todas las agencias de viajes de Hanoi y Saigón pueden organizar un tur individualizado del país en automóvil privado, con chofer y traductor guía. El costo por kilómetro varía desde los 30 a los 70 centavos de dolar americano, lo cual depende del tamaño del vehículo. Puede que uno tenga o no que pagar los salarios del guía y del chofer (quizás 5 dólares americanos al día por persona), más el costo de su alojamiento y comidas – valdría la pena clarificar estas cosas antes de comenzar el tur. En muchos casos le darán una cotización por día que lo incluye todo, lo que también

incluye alojamiento en un hotel barato. Aunque no es obligatorio, si el chofer y el guía brindan un buen servicio, ellos agradecerán mucho cualquier propina.

En Bicicleta

Es muy posible recorrer Vietnam en bicicleta. El mayor desafío es el planear una ruta que evite el tráfico mortal. Las zonas que se deben evitar incluyen el Delta del Mekong y la Autopista Nacional 1.

Muchos ciclistas quedan completamente cautivados por la Autopista 14 que recorre todas las Tierras Altas Centrales del sur (alrededor de Buon Ma Thuot). La Autopista 7, que va desde Hanoi hasta la frontera

con China en Lao Cai, también recibe buenas recomendaciones.

Se pueden comprar bicicletas de baja calidad de tipo montaña en Hanoi y Saigón, pero la mayoría de los ciclistas prefieren traer sus propias bicicletas.

En Bote

Los viajes largos en bote son los más prácticos en el Delta del Mekong de la región sur de Vietnam ya que lo cruzan cientos de ríos y canales. Sin embargo, existen tures populares panorámicos de un día en los que se puede visitar las islas cercanas a la costa, especialmente en Nha Trang y en la Bahía Halong.

RICHARD I'ANSON

ROBERT STOREY

Top: Trading on the river, Mytho, Mekong Delta
Bottom: Grotto, Halong Bay

ベトナムの旅

日本語
バス

ベトナムを旅行する者にとって喜ばしいことは、バスの運賃が大変安く、広範囲にわたって路線網が発達しており、国内のいたるところに行けるということだ。だが欠点は、遅れがちで混雑しており、乗り心地も悪い上、よく故障する。バスの運転手は、目的地に着くあいだじゅう、頻繁に乗客の乗り降りのためにバスを止める。このため、よく時刻に遅れるが、いらだたせられる理由はそれだけではない。バスは目的地に近づくにつれ、次第に混んでくる。理論的に言えば、二人分の乗車券を買って一人で悠々と足を伸ばせるはずなのだが、実際には他の乗客が押し寄せてくるので、自分の場所を確保するのに気をもまなくてはいけない。車内には荷物置き場がほとんどなく、バスの屋根に荷物を積み込むことになるが、そうすると、走行中荷物からものを取り出せなくなるので注意すること。

もう一つの交通手段としてミニバスがある。こちらはバスよりも乗り心地が良く速い。ミニバスには公営のものとチャーター用のものの二種類がある。公営のミニバスは前述の大型バスの縮小版と思っていい。目的地に着くあいだ、乗客を拾い続けるので大変込み合い、楽ではない。チャーター用のミニバスは余分な乗客を乗せてはいけないことになっているが、もちろんその分料金は高くなる。チャーター用のミニバスの座席は、喫茶店、ホテル、外国人や裕福なベトナム人がよく利用する旅行代理店で簡単に予約することができる。

電車

ベトナムの鉄道は全長 2600km で、国を南北に貫くハノイとサイゴンを結ぶ路線（1726km）を含めて、ほとんどが単線である。ハノイからさらに三本の支線が分かれている。そのうち二本は中国国境に、もう一本はハイフォン港に延びている。

サイゴンとハノイを結ぶ『再統一急行（Reunification Express）』にはエアコン付きの寝台車がある。しかし、地方の電車は大変遅い上、乗り心地も悪く、盗難の危険性が高い。

座席には様々なクラスがあり、料金は乗り心地具合によりだいぶ差がある。

自動車

ベトナムには、自分で運転するレンタカーはまだ登場していないが、運転手付きのハイヤーや貸し切りのミニバスは大変安いので、交通手段の一つとして考慮に入れておくといい。実際、老朽化したベトナムの公営交通機関の実情を考えると、貸し切りの車を使った旅行に人気が集まるのももっともだ。少人数のグループで料金を割れば、旅行

RICHARD I'ANSON

Cholon Market, Ho Chi Minh City

者一人当たりのコストはさらに
下がる。一日一人当たり US$5
ぐらいで済むこともある。

　ハノイとサイゴンにあるほ
とんどの旅行代理店で、注文に
応じて、個人所有の車と運転手、
ガイドを付けたツアーを組んで
くれる。料金は車の大きさによ
り 1km 当たり US$0.30 から
US$0.70 ほどだ。ツアーの種
類により、ガイドと運転手に日
給（一人当たり約 US$5）、宿
泊費、食費を支払うこともある
が、これらの料金については出
発前に必ず相手とはっきり交渉
すること。ほとんどの場合、見
積もり内に 1 日に必要な料金
（格安の宿泊料込み）がすべて
含まれている。運転手やガイド
のサービスが良い時にはチップ
を渡すことを勧める。

DEANNA SWANEY

自転車
ベトナムを自転車でツアーする
のは十分可能だが、最大のチャ
レンジは、殺人的交通量の多い
危険なルートを避けるための計
画を立てることにあると言って
いい。避けて通るべき地域は、
メコン・デルタと国道 1 号線だ。

　南部の中央高地（バンメ
トート付近）を通る１４号線は
多くのサイクリストを魅了する。
ハノイから中国国境のラオカイ
まで通る 7 号線も評判がいい。

　ハノイとサイゴンでは、質
の悪いマウンテン・バイクが買
えるが、ほとんどのサイクリス
トは自分の自転車を持っていく
のを好むようだ。

ボート
数多くの川や運河が網の目状に
交差しているため、ベトナム南
部のメコン・デルタを旅するに
は、ボートが最も便利だ。また、
沖合にある島を訪れる観光日帰
りツアーもある。特にニャチャ
ン、ハロン湾は人気がある。

DEANNA SWANEY

Top: Gate to Imperial City, Hué
Bottom: Po Klong Garai Cham Towers, near Phan Rang-Thap Cham

Index

Note: to find Beaches; Caves; Churches & Cathedrals; Forts & Citadels; Islands; Mosques; Mountains & Passes; National Parks; Rivers, Lakes & Bays; Ruins; Temples; and Waterfalls see the alphabetical listings under each heading at the end of the general index.

GENERAL INDEX

All places are in Vietnam, except:

Cam = Cambodia
Chi = China
Lao = Laos
Tha = Thailand

For duplicate names in Vietnam, the province abbreviations are:

AG = An Giang
BR = Ba Ria-Vung Tau
BT = Bac Thai
BTr = Ben Tre
BD = Binh Dinh
BTh = Binh Thuan
C = Cantho
CB = Cao Bang
DL = Dac Lac
DN = Dong Nai
DT = Dong Thap
GL = Gia Lai
HB = Ha Bac
HG = Ha Giang
HT = Ha Tay
HTi = Ha Tinh
HH = Hai Hung
HP = Haiphong
HN = Hanoi
HC = Ho Chi Minh
HBi = Hoa Binh
KH = Khanh Hoa
KG = Kien Giang
K = Kon Tum
LC = Lai Chau
LD = Lam Dong
LS = Lang Son
LCa = Lao Cai
LA = Long An
MH = Minh Hai
NH = Nam Ha
NA = Nghe An
NB = Ninh Binh
NT = Ninh Thuan
PY = Phu Yen
QB = Quang Binh
QN = Quang Ngai
QD = Quang Nam Danang
QNi = Quang Ninh
QT = Quang Tri
ST = Soc Trang
SL = Son La
SB = Song Be
TN = Tay Ninh
TB = Thai Binh
TH = Thanh Hoa
TT = Thua Thien-Hué
TG = Tien Giang
TV = Tra Vinh
TQ = Tuyen Quang
VL = Vinh Long
VP = Vinh Phu
YB = Yen Bai

A Dong 21 G6
A Hoi 22 D4
A Le Thiem 22 C2
A Lu 10 D3
A Lum (Lao) 22 C2
A Luong (Lao) 22 C3
A Pa Chai 10 A4
A Ro 22 D4
A Rouye 22 D3
A Shau 22 D3
A Tep 22 D3
A Yun Pa 24 D5
Aluoi 22 C2
An Bien 29 E6
An Dinh 24 D4
An Hai 17 E4
An Hoa (QD) 23 F3
An Hoa (BD) 25 E2
An Hoa (SB) 30 B2
An Hoa (MH) 32 C3
An Khe 24 D4
An Lam 31 F2
An Lao 25 E2
An Leo 17 F2
An Loc 26 A5
An Long 29 F3
An Phu 29 F4
An Phuoc 27 G6
An Thit 30 B4
An Trach 32 C3
Ang Co Chay (Cam) 28 D3
Angtai Som (Cam) 28 D3
Anh Son 18 D3
Ap Bac 29 G4
Ap Ong Lang 28 B5
At Lam (Lao) 20 D6
Attapu (Lao) 22 B6

Ba Be 12 C4
Ba Beo 31 F3
Ba Binh 21 G4
Ba Che 17 G2
Ba Chuc 28 D4
Ba Don 21 E3
Ba Dong 23 G6
Ba Gia 23 G5
Ba Keo 28 B5
Ba Long 21 G6
Ba Na 23 E3
Ba Quan 32 B4
Ba Ria 30 C4
Ba San 13 F5
Ba The 29 E5
Ba Thuoc 16 B5
Ba Ti (Cam) 28 D2
Ba To 23 G6
Ba Tri 30 A5
Ba Vi 16 B3
Bac Binh 31 G2
Bac Chung (Lao) 22 C4
Bac Giang 16 D2
Bac Ha 11 F4
Ba Hon 28 C5
Bac Lieu (MH) 32 D3
Bac Me 12 B3
Bac Moui 17 G2
Bac Ninh 16 D3
Bac Quang 11 H4
Bac Son 13 E5
Bac Yen 15 G2
Bach Coc 16 D5
Bach Ma 23 E2
Bach Thong (Bac Can) 12 C5
Bai Cau 16 B2

Bai Den 19 F2
Bai Duc Thon 20 D2
Bai Thuong 16 B6
Ban Ai Nu 24 D6
Ban Bin 15 H6
Ban Bo 15 G5
Ban Brieng 24 C6
Ban Bung (Lao) 20 D5
Ban Cang (Lao) 20 D4
Ban Cay (Lao) 22 B3
Ban Chat 13 G6
Ban Chong (HG) 11 H3
Ban Chong (NA) 18 D3
Ban Co (Lao) 21 E5
Ban Cong (NA) 18 D2
Ban Cong (NA) 18 D4
Ban Dam 19 E3
Ban Dan 14 C2
Ban Don 26 D2
Ban Dong (Lao) 21 E6
Ban Drang Phok 26 D2
Ban Giay 12 B2
Ban Hai 21 G5
Ban Hang 15 H5
Ban Hao 11 E6
Ban Het 22 D6
Ban Hon 11 E6
Ban Kha Na (Lao) 14 A2
Ban Kho (Lao) 14 C6
Ban Khone Kene (Lao) 20 A6
Ban Klong 27 F4
Ban Lac Duong 27 E4
Ban Lao (Lao) 20 A3
Ban Lao (Lao) 21 E6
Ban Lap 12 C5
Ban Lau 11 F4
Ban Mai (Tha) 18 A6
Ban Muong 11 H2
Ban Na (Lao) 14 A4
Ban Na Ca 18 D3
Ban Na Phok (Lao) 18 B6
Ban Na Tai (Lao) 14 B4
Ban O 11 E6
Ban Pak Sa (Lao) 18 A6
Ban Peng (Lao) 22 B2
Ban Phang 16 B6
Ban Phiet 11 F4
Ban Phon (Lao) 22 B4
Ban Sa San 18 B3
Ban Sai 13 E4
Ban Se (Lao) 14 C5
Ban Sop Tioc (Lao) 14 B5
Ban Tang 22 D6
Ban Thach 25 F6
Ban Thana (Lao) 18 A6
Ban Trap 24 C6
Ban Tung 27 F2
Ban Tuong 27 G3
Ban Van (Lao) 20 B5
Ban Xa Thu 24 D6
Ban Xop Nam 18 C4
Banam (Cam) 29 E2
Bang Muong 15 H2
Bangun (Chi) 13 G5
Banli (Chi) 13 H5
Bao Ha 11 G5
Bao Lac 12 C2
Bao Loc 26 D6
Bao Yen 11 G5
Bat Xat 11 E4
Bau Long 26 A6
Bau Tram 29 H1
Ben Cat 30 A2
Ben Cui 29 H2

Ben Luc 30 A4
Ben Nhurt 29 E6
Ben Pha 33 E2
Ben Quang 21 F5
Ben Suc 29 H2
Ben Thuy 19 F5
Ben Tre 29 H5
Ben Triem 21 E4
Bet Chan Da (Cam) 26 C2
Bich Son 26 D5
Bien Hoa 30 B3
Bim Son 16 C6
Bin Chanh 30 A4
Bin Hung 29 E4
Binh Chau 30 D4
Binh Dai 30 B5
Binh Dinh 25 E4
Binh Gia (LS) 13 E5
Binh Gia (BR) 30 C4
Binh Khuong 23 G5
Binh Lam 31 F3
Binh Lieu 17 G2
Binh Long 16 D6
Binh Lu 11 E4
Binh Luc 16 D5
Binh Minh 29 G5
Bo Dau 12 C6
Bo Ha 16 D2
Bo Kham (Cam) 24 A4
Bo Trach 21 E3
Bokor Hill Station (Cam) 28 B4
Bon Bu Tong 26 D4
Bong Ca Xen (Lao) 20 A4
Bong Mieu 23 F4
Bu Blim 26 B4
Bu Dang 26 C5
Bu Dop 26 A4
Bu Gia Map 26 B4
Bu Go 26 C5
Bu Na 26 B5
Bu Nho 26 A5
Bu Prang 26 B4
Bu Xa 26 B4
Bua La Pha (Lao) 20 C4
Buan Ya Sou 24 B6
Buon Ma Thuot 27 E2
Buon Sop 26 D5
Buon Thach Troi 27 G4
Buon Tur 26 D3
Buy Phloc (Cam) 26 A3

Ca Lang 10 B4
Ca Long (Lao) 18 D5
Ca Lu 21 F6
Ca Na 27 G6
Ca Vac (Lao) 20 C4
Ca Vinh 11 H6
Ca Xeng 20 C2
Cai Be 29 G4
Cai Cai 29 F3
Cai Keo 32 B4
Cai Lay 29 G4
Cai Mon 29 H5
Cai Nuoc 32 B4
Cai Rang 29 G5
Cai San 29 E5
Cam Binh 17 E3
Cam Duong 11 F4
Cam Lo 21 G5
Cam My 30 C3
Cam Pha 17 G3
Cam Ranh 27 H5
Cam Thuy 16 B5
Cam Xuyen 19 G6

Bamboo Island (Hon Tre) 27 H4
Bay Canh Island 33 G4
Bo Han Island (Ile de la Surprise) 17 G4
Cat Ba Island 17 G4
Cau Island 33 G4
Cham Island 23 G3
Con Co 21 G4
Con Dao Islands 33 F4
Con Son Island 33 F4
Cu Lao Re 23 H4
Cu Lao Xanh 25 F5
Dao Cai Bao 17 H3
Dao Cai Chien 17 G6, 17 H2
Dao Co To 17 H3
Dao Dong Khoa 17 H3
Dao Ha Mai 17 H4
Dao Long Chau 17 G4
Dao Nghi Son 19 F3
Dao Ngoc Vung 17 G4
Dao Quan Lan 17 H4
Dao Sau Nam 17 H3
Dao Tra Ban 17 H3
Dao Trao 17 G3
Dao Vinh Thuc 17 G6
Dau Be Island 17 G4
Hang Dau Go Island (Ile des Merveilles) 17 F3
Hang Trai Island (Ile de l'Union) 17 F4
Hon Chala 27 H3
Hon Chuoi 32 A4
Hon Cohe 25 F4
Hon Gom Peninsula 27 H3
Hon Heo 27 H3
Hon Mau 28 C6
Hon Me 19 G3
Hon Mieu 27 H4
Hon Minh Hoa 28 C5
Hon Mun 27 H4
Hon Nam Du 28 C6
Hon Ne Island 16 D6
Hon Noi 27 H4
Hon Rai 28 C6
Hon Sao 32 A5
Hon Sau 28 C6
Hon Tam 27 H4
Hon Trau 25 F3
Hon Truoc 28 C6
Lao Dua 25 F6
Lao Ma Nha 25 F6
Nghi Son Islands 19 G3
Ong Island 23 G3
Poulo Dama 28 C6
Pulo Panjang 28 A6
Rocher Table Island 28 B6
Rocky Island (Hon Buong) 32 A4
Roi Island 28 B6
Set Island (Cam) 28 A4
Son Cha Island 23 F2
Stag's Head Peninsula 28 C4
Tham Island 28 B6
Thmei Island (Cam) 28 A4
Tho Island 33 F4
Trac Island 33 F4
Tre Lon Island 33 F4
Tre Nho Island 33 F4
Trung Lon Island 33 E5
Trung Nho Island 33 E5
Vung Island 33 F4

MOSQUES

Chau Giang Mosque (Chau Doc) 29 E3
Cholon Mosque (HCM) 30 B3
Former Indian Mosque (Hué) 21 H6
Saigon Central Mosque 30 B3

MOUNTAINS & PASSES

An Khe Pass 24 D4
Ba Vi 16 B3
Cao Veou 18 D4
Cham Chu 11 H5
Chao Mountain 28 B4
Chu Don 26 C2
Chu Kling 24 B6
Chu Nhon 25 E5
Chu Pong 24 A5
Chu Rpan 24 C4
Cu Mong Pass 25 F4
Deo Ngang (Ngang Pass) 21 E2
Elephant 12 D5
Elephant Mountains (Cam) 28 B1, 28 B3
Fansipan 11 E4
Hai Van Pass 23 F2
Ham Rong Mountain 28 B4
Hoang Lien Mountains 11 E5, 11 F5, 11 F6
Hon Ba 23 F5
Jeying Ling (Chi) 17 H5
Ked Nua Pass 19 E6
Kiou Leou Ti 11 G3
Kon Borla 24 C3
La San (Lao) 10 A4
Lang Bian Mountain 27 F4
Lang Cung 11 F5
Laochun Shan (Chi) 11 E1
Marble Mountains 23 F3
Moc Bai Border Crossing 29 H2
Mu Gia Pass (Lao) 20 C3
Nam Mau 17 F3
Nam Mountain 27 H4
Nam Vap 17 G3
Ngoan Muc Pass 27 F5
Ngoc Chua 23 G5
Ngoc Linh Mountain 23 E5
Nui Ba Den (Black Lady Mountain) 29 H1
Nui Ba Mu (Lao) 18 D5
Nui Ong 31 E2
Nui Son Tra 23 F2
Pha Luong 15 G4
Phou Lap 15 H3
Phou Loi (Lao) 14 C5
Phou Loupe (Lao) 15 G5
Phou Pane (Lao) 15 F5
Phou Tia Lao Pie (Lao) 10 A6
Phoung Chang 11 E3
Phu Lai Lang 18 B3
Phu Pha Pet (Lao) 18 B6
Phu Set (Lao) 22 A4
Pou Nam Ke 10 A5
Rao Co (Lao) 19 E6
Sam Sao 14 D4
Truong Son Mountains (Lao) 20 C2, 20 C4, 20 D4
Truong Son Mountains 18 C4, 18 D5, 19 E6
Tsi Con Ling 11 H3
Vo Quap Mountain 28 B5

NATIONAL PARKS

Ba Be Lake National Park 12 C4
Bach Ma National Park 23 E2
Camau Nature Reserve 32 B4
Cat Ba National Park 17 F4
Cuc Phuong National Park 16 C5
Nam Cat Tien National Park 26 C5

RIVERS, LAKES & BAYS

Ba Be Lake 12 C4
Ba Kr Nanna 27 E3
Bai Khem Point 28 B5
Bai Sao Point 28 B5
Bay of Danang 23 F2
Ben Hai River 21 F5
Black River 10 D6
Ca Map Point 33 F4
Ca Mau Cape 32 A5
Ca Pass 27 H2
Cam Ranh Bay 27 H5
Cape An Hoa 23 G4
Cape Bang 19 F3
Cape Batangan 23 H5
Cape Chan May Dong 23 E2
Cape Danang 23 F2
Cape Falaise 19 F4
Cape Faux Varella 27 H5
Cape Hirondelles 25 F4
Cape Lay 21 G4
Cape Mui Ron 19 H6
Cape Mui Sot 19 G5
Cape Nam Tram 23 H4
Cape Padaran 27 G6
Cau 12 D6
Cay Duong Bay 28 D5
Chao Bay 25 F5
Claire (Chi) 11 H2
Claire 12 B6
Cung-Hau Bay 30 B6
Da Chong Point 28 B4
Da Dung 27 E5
Da Te 26 C6
Dac Lac Lake 27 E3
Dai Giang 21 E4
Dak Bla 24 C2
Dak Dam (Cam) 26 C3
Dak Dein 23 F6
Dak Deung 26 C5
Dak Glun 26 B5
Dak Kroeng (Cam) 26 A2
Dak Plai (Cam) 26 C2
Dak Poyo (Lao) 22 C4
Dak Rlap 26 B5
Dak Rouei (Cam) 26 B1
Dakrong River 21 F6
Dam Cau Hai 23 E2
Dan Nhim 27 F5
Dan Nhim Lake 27 F5
Dat Do Point 28 B5
Dau Tieng Lake 29 H2
Day 16 C4
Den Phach Point 28 B5
Dong Ho 28 C4
Dong Nai 26 C6, 30 B3
Dung Quat Bay 23 G4
Duong 16 D3
Ea H'leo 24 B5
Ea Krong (Cam) 26 C1
Ea Krong Aa 24 A6
East Vaico 29 H3
Fat Tai Long Bay 17 G3
Ganh Dau Point 28 A4
Ganh Rai Bay 30 B5
Ha Giao 25 E3
Halong Bay 17 G3
Hanh Point 28 B5
Hau Giang (Bassac) (Cam) 29 E2
Hau Giang (Bassac) 29 F5, 33 E2
Heishui He (Chi) 13 G4
Hoi Bay 19 F4
Hon Mat 19 F5
Ia Anhh 24 C4
Ke Ga Point 31 E3
Kien Giang 21 F4
Kim 11 F6
Kompong Som Bay (Cam) 28 A3
Krong Hnang 27 F2
Krong Poko 22 D6
Kwala Point 28 B4
Lake Tri An 30 C2
Langa Lake 30 C2
Long Song 27 F6, 31 G2
Longxu He 13 E1
Mekong Delta 30 A6
Mekong River (Lao) 14 A6, 20 A6
Mong Tay Point 28 A5
Mouths of the Mekong 30 B6
Mui Ne Point 31 F3
Nam Ca Dinh (Lao) 18 B6
Nam Chat (Lao) 18 D5
Nam Giang (Lao) 15 G6
Nam Hang (Lao) 18 B5
Nam Het (Lao) 15 E4
Nam Hung (Lao) 18 D5
Nam Kang (Lao) 10 A5
Nam Khao (Lao) 14 D6
Nam La (Chi) 10 B2
Nam La (Lao) 20 B4
Nam Leng (Lao) 10 A6
Nam Lieon (Cam) 24 A6
Nam Lieon 26 C1
Nam Loi (Lao) 20 B2
Nam Ma 14 D3
Nam Mat (Lao) 18 A2
Nam Mau 11 E5
Nam Mo 18 B3
Nam Mouk 10 D6
Nam Muone (Lao) 18 B5
Nam Na 10 C4
Nam Nhie 10 B5
Nam Nhuong (Lao) 18 D6
Nam Noua (Lao) 14 C2
Nam Nun 23 E5
Nam One (Lao) 20 B3
Nam Ou (Lao) 14 A6
Nam Ou (Lao) 14 B3
Nam Pak (Lao) 14 A4
Nam Pang (Lao) 18 A6
Nam Pha Nang (Lao) 20 C4
Nam Phao (Lao) 18 D6
Nam Sam (Lao) 15 F6
Nam Seuang (Lao) 14 C5
Nam Sot (Lao) 20 B2
Nam Ten (Lao) 14 C6
Nam Theun (Lao) 18 D6
Nam Theun (Lao) 20 B2
Nam Tiouen (Lao) 18 B4
Nam Tse (Lao) 20 D4
Nanhai He (Chi) 11 E3
Nan Sane (Lao) 18 A5
Ngan Pho 19 E5
Ngan Sau 19 F6
Ngoi Hut 11 G6
Ngoi Nhu 11 F5
Ngoi Thie 11 G6
Nguon Nan 20 D3
Nguon Nay 20 D2
Nin Jiang (Chi) 13 H5
Ong Doi Point 28 B5
Padaran Bay 27 G6
Perfume River 22 D2
Phan Ri Bay 31 G2
Phan Thiet Bay 31 F3
Point Hon Nei 27 H4
Pou Din Dinh 10 B5
Prek Tate (Cam) 29 F1
Prek Thnot (Cam) 28 B1
Prek Trabek (Cam) 29 F2
Pu Kho Luong 10 D4
Rach Cua Can 28 B4
Rach Giang Thank 28 C4
Rau Nhat 21 F3
Red River (Song Hong) 11 F4
Red River 16 D4
Red River Delta 16 D4, 17 E4
Se Bang Fai (Lao) 20 A5, 20 C3
Se Bang Hieng (Lao) 21 E5
Se Champhone (Lao) 20 B6
Se Kamane (Lao) 22 C5
Se Kong (Lao) 22 B4

LONELY PLANET TV SERIES & VIDEOS

Lonely Planet travel guides have been brought to life on television screens around the world. Like our guides, the programmes are based on the joy of independent travel, and look honestly at some of the most exciting, picturesque and frustrating places in the world. Each show is presented by one of three travellers from Australia, England or the USA and combines an innovative mixture of video, Super-8 film, atmospheric soundscapes and original music.

Videos of each episode – containing additional footage not shown on television – are available from good book and video shops, but the availability of individual videos varies with regional screening schedules.

Video destinations include:
Alaska; Australia (Southeast); Brazil; Ecuador & the Galapagos Islands; Indonesia; Israel & the Sinai Desert; Japan; La Ruta Maya (Yucatan, Guatemala & Belize); Morocco; North India (Varanasi to the Himalaya); Pacific Islands; Vietnam; Zimbabwe, Botswana & Namibia.

Coming in 1996:
The Arctic (Norway & Finland); Baja California; Chile & Easter Island; China (Southeast); Costa Rica; East Africa (Tanzania & Zanzibar); Great Barrier Reef (Australia); Jamaica; Papua New Guinea; the Rockies (USA); Syria & Jordan; Turkey.

The Lonely Planet television series is produced by:
Pilot Productions
Duke of Sussex Studios,
44 Uxbridge St,
London W8 7TG, UK

Lonely Planet videos are distributed by:
IVN Communications Inc
2246 Camino Ramon, San Ramon,
California 94583, USA

107 Power Road, Chiswick,
London W4 5PL, UK

PLANET TALK
Lonely Planet's FREE quarterly newsletter

We love hearing from you and think you'd like to hear from us.
When...is the right time to see reindeer in Finland?
Where...can you hear the best palm-wine music in Ghana?
How...do you get from Asunción to Areguá by steam train?
What...is the best way to see India?

For the answer to these and many other questions read PLANET TALK.

Every issue is packed with up-to-date travel news and advice including:

- a letter from Lonely Planet founders Tony and Maureen Wheeler
- travel diary from a Lonely Planet author – find out what it's really like out on the road
- feature article on an important and topical travel issue
- a selection of recent letters from our readers
- the latest travel news from all over the world
- details on Lonely Planet's new and forthcoming releases

To join our mailing list contact any Lonely Planet office.

Also available: Lonely Planet T-shirts. 100% heavyweight cotton (S, M, L, XL).

LONELY PLANET GUIDEBOOKS

Lonely Planet guidebooks are distributed worldwide.They are also available by mail order from Lonely Planet, so if you have difficulty finding a title please write to us. US and Canadian residents should write to Embarcadero West, 155 Filbert St, Suite 251, Oakland CA 94607, USA ; European residents should write to 10 Barley Mow Passage, Chiswick, London W4 4PH; and residents of other countries to PO Box 617, Hawthorn, Victoria 3122, Australia.

NORTH-EAST ASIA
Beijing city guide • China • Cantonese phrasebook • Mandarin Chinese phrasebook • Hong Kong, Macau & Canton • Japan • Japanese phrasebook • Korea • Korean phrasebook • Mongolia • Mongolian phrasebook • North-East Asia on a shoestring • Seoul city guide • Taiwan • Tibet • Tibet phrasebook • Tokyo city guide

INDIAN SUBCONTINENT
Bangladesh • Bengali phrasebook • India • India & Bangladesh travel atlas • Hindi/Urdu phrasebook • Trekking in the Indian Himalaya • Karakoram Highway • Kashmir, Ladakh & Zanskar • Nepal • Trekking in the Nepal Himalaya • Nepali phrasebook • Pakistan • Sri Lanka • Sri Lanka phrasebook

EUROPE
Baltic States & Kaliningrad • Baltics States phrasebook • Britain • Central Europe on a shoestring • Central Europe phrasebook • Czech & Slovak Republics • Dublin city guide • Eastern Europe on a shoestring • Eastern Europe phrasebook • Finland • France • Greece • Greek phrasebook • Hungary • Iceland, Greenland & the Faroe Islands • Ireland • Italy • Mediterranean Europe on a shoestring • Mediterranean Europe phrasebook • Poland • Prague city guide • Scandinavian & Baltic Europe on a shoestring • Scandinavian Europe phrasebook • Slovenia • Switzerland • Trekking in Greece • Trekking in Spain • USSR • Russian phrasebook • Vienna city guide • Western Europe on a shoestring • Western Europe phrasebook

NORTH AMERICA & MEXICO
Alaska • Backpacking in Alaska • Baja California • Canada • Hawaii • Honolulu city guide • Mexico • Pacific Northwest USA • Rocky Mountain States • Southwest USA • USA phrasebook

SOUTH-EAST ASIA
Bali & Lombok • Bangkok city guide • Cambodia • Indonesia • Indonesian phrasebook • Indonesian audio pack • Ho Chi Minh City guide • Jakarta city guide • Java • Laos • Lao phrasebook • Malaysia, Singapore & Brunei • Myanmar (Burma) • Burmese phrasebook • Philippines • Pilipino phrasebook • Singapore city guide • South-East Asia on a shoestring • Thailand • Thailand travel atlas • Thai phrasebook • Thai Hill Tribes phrasebook • Thai audio pack • Vietnam • Vietnamese phrasebook • Vietnamese audio pack • Vietnam travel atlas

AUSTRALIA & THE PACIFIC
Australia • Australian phrasebook • Bushwalking in Australia • Islands of Australia's Great Barrier Reef • Outback Australia • Fiji • Fijian phrasebook • Melbourne city guide • Micronesia • New Caledonia • New South Wales & the ACT • New Zealand • Tramping in New Zealand • Papua New Guinea • Bushwalking in Papua New Guinea • Papua New Guinea phrasebook • Queensland • Rarotonga & the Cook Islands • Samoa • Solomon Islands • Sydney city guide • Tahiti & French Polynesia • Tonga • Vanuatu • Victoria • Western Australia

MIDDLE EAST
Arab Gulf States • Egypt & the Sudan • Arabic (Egyptian) phrasebook • Iran • Israel • Jordan & Syria • Middle East • Turkey • Turkish phrasebook • Trekking in Turkey • Yemen

SOUTH AMERICA
Argentina, Uruguay & Paraguay • Bolivia • Brazil • Brazilian phrasebook • Chile & Easter Island • Colombia • Ecuador & the Galápagos Islands • Latin American Spanish phrasebook • Peru • Quechua phrasebook • Rio de Janeiro city guide • South America on a shoestring • Trekking in the Patagonian Andes • Venezuela

AFRICA
Africa on a shoestring • Central Africa • East Africa • Trekking in East Africa • Kenya • Swahili phrasebook • Morocco • Arabic (Moroccan) phrasebook • North Africa • South Africa, Lesotho & Swaziland • West Africa • Zimbabwe, Botswana & Namibia • Zimbabwe, Botswana & Namibia travel atlas

ISLANDS OF THE INDIAN OCEAN
Madagascar & Comoros • Maldives & Islands of the East Indian Ocean • Mauritius, Réunion & Seychelles

CENTRAL AMERICA & THE CARIBBEAN
Central America on a shoestring • Costa Rica • Eastern Caribbean • Guatemala, Belize & Yucatán: La Ruta Maya

ALSO AVAILABLE FROM LONELY PLANET

Vietnam – a travel survival kit

From the wide avenues and pavement restaurants of Hanoi and Saigon to the spectacular verdant countryside, travelling in Vietnam is packed with challenges and surprises. A comprehensive and informative guide to one of the region's most popular destinations.

Ho Chi Minh City guide

Set in the lush tropical lowlands of south Vietnam, Ho Chi Minh City is a city full of colour – enchanting pagodas and temples, bustling markets and abundant nightlife. This comprehensive guide will help you enjoy it all.

Vietnamese phrasebook

Vietnamese is a vibrant language and even a little knowledge will help visitors to gain an understanding of Vietnamese culture as well as make many friends along the way.

Vietnamese audio pack

Join two travellers as they visit Vietnam – meeting local people, finding accommodation, eating out and sightseeing.

Travellers will learn essential words and phrases – and their correct pronunciation – by participating in a realistic story. The scripts have been developed in the belief that the best way to learn a new language is to hear it, then to practise it in the context in which you will use it. The emphasis is on effective communication.

Using the phrasebook as a reference, you'll find essential words and phrases, notes on grammar, cultural tips and plenty of vocabulary.

Audio packs are an innovative combination of a cassette/CD and phrasebook presented in an attractive cloth wallet made from indigenous textiles by local community groups in the countries where the languages are spoken.

Features of the cassettes & CDs:
- realistic storylines explore situations that will be useful for all travellers
- languages are spoken by native speakers
- listeners learn key words and phrases in repetition exercises, then hear them used in context
- realistic sound effects and indigenous music used throughout
- length: 80-90 minutes

OTHER LONELY PLANET TRAVEL ATLASES

India & Bangladesh

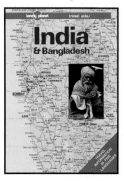

Thailand

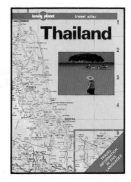

Zimbabwe, Botswana & Namibia

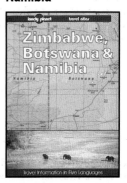

THE LONELY PLANET STORY

Lonely Planet published its first book in 1973 in response to the numerous 'How did you do it?' questions Maureen and Tony Wheeler were asked after driving, bussing, hitching, sailing and railing their way from England to Australia.

Written at a kitchen table and hand collated, trimmed and stapled, *Across Asia on the Cheap* became an instant local bestseller, inspiring thoughts of another book.

Eighteen months in South-East Asia resulted in their second guide, *South-East Asia on a shoestring*, which they put together in a backstreet Chinese hotel in Singapore in 1975. The 'yellow bible', as it quickly became known to backpackers around the world, soon became *the* guide to the region. It has sold well over half a million copies and is now in its 8th edition, still retaining its familiar yellow cover.

Today there are over 140 Lonely Planet titles in print – books that have that same adventurous approach to travel as those early guides; books that 'assume you know how to get your luggage off the carousel' as one reviewer put it.

Although Lonely Planet initially specialised in guides to Asia, they now cover most regions of the world, including the Pacific, South America, Africa, the Middle East and Europe. The list of *walking guides* and *phrasebooks* (for 'unusual' languages such as Quechua, Swahili, Nepali and Egyptian Arabic) is also growing rapidly.

The emphasis continues to be on travel for independent travellers. Tony and Maureen still travel for several months of each year and play an active part in the writing, updating and quality control of Lonely Planet's guides.

They have been joined by over 50 authors, 110 staff – mainly editors, cartographers & designers – at our office in Melbourne, Australia, at our US office in Oakland, California and at our European office in Paris; another five at our office in London handle sales for Britain, Europe and Africa. Travellers themselves also make a valuable contribution to the guides through the feedback we receive in thousands of letters each year.

The people at Lonely Planet strongly believe that travellers can make a positive contribution to the countries they visit, both through their appreciation of the countries' culture, wildlife and natural features, and through the money they spend. In addition, the company makes a direct contribution to the countries and regions it covers. Since 1986 a percentage of the income from each book has been donated to ventures such as famine relief in Africa; aid projects in India; agricultural projects in Central America; Greenpeace's efforts to halt French nuclear testing in the Pacific; and Amnesty International.

Lonely Planet's basic travel philosophy is summed up in Tony Wheeler's comment, 'Don't worry about whether your trip will work out. Just go!'.

LONELY PLANET PUBLICATIONS

AUSTRALIA (HEAD OFFICE)
PO Box 617, Hawthorn
3122, Victoria
tel: (03) 9819 1877
fax: (03) 9819 6459
e-mail: talk2us@lonelyplanet.com.au

USA
Embarcadero West,
155 Filbert St, Suite 251,
Oakland, CA 94607
tel: (510) 893 8555   TOLL FREE: 800 275-8555
fax: (510) 893 8563
e-mail: info@lonelyplanet.com

UK
10 Barley Mow Passage,
Chiswick, W4 4PH, London
tel: (0181) 742 3161
fax: (0181) 742 2772
e-mail: 100413.3551@compuserve.com

FRANCE
71 bis rue du Cardinal Lemoine
75005 Paris
tel: 1 46 34 00 58
fax: 1 46 34 72 55
e-mail: 100560.415@compuserve.com

World Wide Web: http://www.lonelyplanet.com/

Notes